Seasons of Mangoes and Brainfire

Also by Carolyne Wright

Books of Poetry
Stealing the Children
Premonitions of an Uneasy Guest
A Change of Maps

Chapbooks
Returning What We Owed
From a White Woman's Journal
Brief Irreveries
Carolyne Wright: Greatest Hits, 1975–2001

Translations
In Order to Talk with the Dead:
Selected Poems of Jorge Teillier
(from the Spanish)
The Game in Reverse:
Poems by Taslima Nasrin
(from the Bengali)
Another Spring, Darkness:
Selected Poems of Anuradha Mahapatra
(from the Bengali)

Nonfiction
A Choice of Fidelities:
Lectures and Readings from a Writer's Life

Seasons of
Mangoes and Brainfire

Poems by

Carolyne Wright

A Lynx House Book

Eastern Washington University Press

First edition published by Lynx House Press, 2000

Page design by Joelean Copeland
Cover design by Christine Holbert
Cover art: "Camelia," oil on wood, by Mary Josephson

Library of Congress Cataloging-in-Publication Data

Wright, Carolyne
   Seasons of mangoes and brainfire : poems / by Carolyne Wright.
     p. cm.
   "A Lynx House book."
   Includes bibliographical references (p.   ).
   ISBN 1-59766-005-1 (pbk. : alk. paper)
   I. Title.
  PS3573.R498S43 2005
  811'.54--dc22

                2005004438

Eastern Washington University Press
Spokane and Cheney, Washington

CONTENTS

I.   *Seasons of Mangoes and Brainfire*

My Last Night in Bahia   / 3
The Conjure Woman   / 6
Survivalist   / 8
After Forty Years   / 9
The Miracle Room   / 11
Wander Luís   / 13
The Opening Up, 1972   / 17
La Push   / 19
Aymara Woman on Socabaya Street   / 22
Eugenia   / 24
The Grade School Teacher During Recess   / 27
Victor Jara (1932–1973)   / 28
Survivor's Story   / 30
Sierra Walk   / 32
The Retarded Woman on Cooper Street   / 34
Harumi   / 36
Post-Revolutionary Letter   / 39
Coplas for Violeta Parra (1917–1967)   / 41
KZ   / 44
The Hammerer   / 46
The Room   / 49
The Peace Corps Volunteer Comes Home   / 52
Message to César Vallejo   / 53
Josie Bliss, October 1971   / 55

II.   *Flowers in Winter*

Flowers in Winter   / 61

Notes on the Poems   / 73
About the Author   / 79
Acknowledgments   / 81

In memory of my father, Maurice C. Wright
and of my mother, Marian L. Wright
for Jim

I

Seasons of Mangoes and Brainfire

"... if they call, we reply:
"I am here," knowing we are not,
that which once was, was and is lost,
is lost in the past, and now will not return."

—Pablo Neruda, "The Past"
translated from the Spanish by Alastair Reid

My Last Night in Bahia

I sat in the Mercado Modelo
drinking rum and pineapple,
waiting all afternoon on a promise—
Eric the Dutch poet, the self-
declared expatriate, gone AWOL
in eight languages from his country's
national service, refusing
to let me take his picture
on steps of the Bomfim church.

Was he casing shops in the square
where we'd danced all night
in crowds maddened by *cachaça*
and the *samba* superstars
making love to their guitars
upon the Carnaval sound trucks?
Was he back at the hotel
where I'd followed once, where
he came down hours later with Gilsinha?

In the spendthrift sun of the market,
I watched *capoeira* players
turn their dream-slow cartwheels,
turbanned women call out
the responses, the *berimbāu*
moan on its one string.

I wore scarlet headscarves
and gold hoops in my ears,
lived on coffee and passion fruit,
street slang and the nervous
lassitude of the dancers.
I'd never fit in.

What lies did I tell myself
nights on my back in the driftwood-
littered sand of Porto da Barra?
The fisherman who stumbled over us
shaking his net-knife, shouting
"*Pimp! Puta!*" until we clambered
trembling, clutching our scattered
clothing, to our feet.

Salt grit between our thighs
all the way back in the streetcar,
cockfights and the syncopated whistles
from the *samba* schools
pierced through my room's thin walls
as he thrust into me again
and again to finish what we'd started.

What about dawn's sudden gusts
of confetti, the clown suit
in a doorway during a sudden downpour
who grabbed Eric's beard and yelled
"*Unmask!*"?

My thoughts were too far gone.
What did the conjure woman tell me
when the glare from the glass ball
shone on her face through cigarette smoke?
Was it a blessing or a curse?
When the spell wore off
I stumbled alone down Ash Wednesday's
abandoned, trash-filled streets.

Then Celso da Costa was beside me—
quiet, slim, the West Coast
of Africa in his skin.
Celso the sidewalk artist
on the outskirts of our little group.
People stared as we danced
the circle *samba*.
"Who expects them to understand?"

He offered his parents' house
for the night, no need to explain
what no one can pay back to another.
A pink stucco cottage behind the square,
blue doors to keep out the bad eye,
sweet herbs in the garden.
One long whitewashed room,
pictures of saints on the walls.

I was ashamed of my hesitation.
After beans and rice and oranges
they gave me the one big bed,
Celso and his brothers on the floor,
his parents behind the kitchen curtain.
The night returning me to myself,
I emptied my pouches of conjure powders.

In the morning, the early bus
back to Rio, and Celso gave me
a painting—a house with blue shutters,
a garden, a dark-skinned family
waving goodbye in the doorway,
their faces full of what
almost could have kept me.

The Conjure Woman

(São Salvador da Bahia)

She blows on the crystal ball,
tells me I can have anything.
Hibiscus flowers.
Jacarandá-wood charms.
A powder from the Mercado Modelo
that drives men wild.

In the waiting room, the man I want
drums his fingers, makes eyes
at the honey-colored woman
stirring something in the kitchen.
Strands of blue pearls,
passion-flower *lenço* on her head.
A little *samba* on the red floor tiles.
Yemanjá, sea goddess,
smiles and waves her fish tail
from the poster on the wall.

The conjure woman turns her wedding rings
around a long story about the sea.
Bahia dialect—the hushed syllables,
palm trees reflecting
on the water, whole sentences
I want to understand.

Samba school drums at the corners,
cachaça bottles passed around.
Women singing the Carnaval tune
Não se esqueça de mim.
Don't leave me, don't forget.
My future—full of missing words,
eavesdropping at the tables
of the deaf, late afternoon
smell of exhaustion.

He's gone. Lady Yemanjá laughs
in the room above the kitchen.
I cross the conjure woman's palm
and go out. The whole town
is in the streets, masked dancers
drumming their true names
from continents that still would fit

together—embracing face to face
like lovers in the salt and sweat
of their sea-displacing passion.
Fishermen drag in their nets
and fall to their knees between
the silver thighs of women.

Survivalist

The rifle's beside you like a lover
when I crawl into bed. The barrel
gleams in the dark, an acceptable
emotion. Boxes of ammo shells
by the nightstand are unconditional
terms for love. You say

your aim's not calculated,
not a bargain struck with a father
training his misaligned sights
on you, cocking the hammer
of his numbered days,

but your personal myth—the basement
stocked with survival rations
for a world you swear
you're not a child of.
Every catalogue you open
subtracts early death
like a row of bull's-eyes
from its discount price.

I flip the light switch on.
Your eyes blink dreams back
for the showdown: a Socrates
hated unto hemlock, a Peter
crucified head down for love. Already

I am one of the survivors.

After Forty Years

"Don't tell me about the bones of Mengele,
the bones are alive and well."
—Michael Dennis Browne

They've found the body
of the Angel of Death,
a bundle of brown bones
and scraps of skin
tossed like market produce
in the gravedigger's tray.

He can be himself now
for his loved ones—those
who took no chances
with the forged passports, bribes,
code words filing past the censors,
never breaking the family silence.

Himself now, for those
whose mouths gaped on silence,
survivors staring through barbed wire
in the abandoned camps,
stumbling chance their messenger,
those for whom the bones
will always be alive and well.

Finally, the tribunal of Embú,
plain light of the TV anchor's day.
Cameras cross-haired on the throats
of witnesses who shrugged
and said nothing, while for years
ash drift, fosses of lime,
the dead kept listening.

He was never sorry.
Death had grown old by the end,
familiar with his dreams:
water burning blue
off the coast of Brazil
like gas jets turned on full.

Strange how the bones are blameless,
the body dissolved as anyone's—
those who walked into the flames
with the prayer for the dead in their mouths,
the angel in his name
passing over the gates of the camps.

The Miracle Room

*(Nosso Senhor do Bomfim Church:
São Salvador da Bahia)*

The Kodaks focus
on the ceiling, a Baroque
reliquary, doll factory
of arms and legs. Facsimiles
the grateful make of ghost limbs
raised from the dead, silver medals
from the mouths of infants
who weren't supposed to live.
Before-and-after photos, testimonies
scotch-taped for years to the wall.
The home-movie makers
check their light meters
and wonder what's held up the tour bus.
They don't notice the little girl
who comes in through the side door
without a face.
They don't see her cross herself,
dip her fingers in holy water
with coupons from the Bahia Hilton
floating on its surface.
No one notices her slide
along the wall, finding her way
with the help of plaster hands
that catch hold of hers.
The charter group doesn't know
she's lighting a candle, kneeling
before Our Lord of Facelessness,
Our Lord of Bomfim.
They can't see the black madonnas
in their sea-froth lace
nod from the altars,
raise carved hands in blessing.

Not even the Cooks' Tours guide
reciting from the souvenir brochures
glances over to see her rise,
blink, sneeze once, press fingers
to the deep rose of her mouth,
and skip out the chapel door,
swinging a mask
from which the features
have been erased.

Wander Luís

(Ouro Prêto, Brasil)

We walk to the top of São Francisco
and huddle under the portico
of the red-tile and soapstone church
while afternoon rain washes away footsteps
of police. "They got my brother
first," you say. "We found his body
in the high grass, bound hand and foot
and blindfolded." *Suicide*,
the uniform at the guard post
shrugged, turning up his soccer game.

You look out past crooked streets
where voices through doorways
chant away the thunder, past
the damp green confusion of hills.
You push dark hair from your eyes,
one hand covers mine
as if tonight your body
could protect me from the story.

Your friends all fled to Chile
in those days: Marcos
in the trunk of the red VW
Regina drove from Rio. Chico Lopes
locked eight months in a closet in Leblon,
lying flat under Guaraní blankets
at the Paraguayan border. Marisa,
pregnant, sobbing in a rented room
in Santiago,
              and you, Wander Luís,
safe in the School of Mines.
The engineering students' *pensão*,
a gallery of blue shuttered doors,
constant trickle of water in the garden.
"What else can I do?" you ask,

three days from anywhere
on the empty highways
of Minas Gerais, between no life
and no other.

You've learned what's precious
in those hills—diamonds and coal
these towns were named for,
stress-tested metals. And occasionally
a glint of sunlight on a thighbone,
the last white flash of understanding
in the cells. What is the atomic weight
of loss? You know your subject.
Father, brother, son. Each name
divided by the blood factor.

"Too many of us live
in doubt's shadow," you say.
Your uncle the graveyard-shift printer,
purple smudges of *samisdat* on his hands
when they came for him.
Your cousin, drilled with M-16 rounds
under the Father of His Country statue.
And you, hitchhiking in Ash Wednesday rain
for the inquest, with drivers
who scarcely knew the language.

How convenient the dead heroes,
after Goulart's and Castelo Branco's madness,
all the blond families friendly
with Stroessner, running the country
like one big *fazênda*, Pôrto Alegre
full of Klaus Barbie connections.

And *Brasil mulato*, laughing and talking
all night, drinking *cachaça* and slave coffee
to forget the parrot perch,
the rubber truncheon, shaved heads
of deportees. Three thousand men
a year who give themselves
to the knife-*samba*, the slow fade

of rain, *favêlas* crumbling on hills
within sight of the Sheratons.

That night, while summer storms
batter the flagstones, I grow
suddenly afraid, ask you to leave.
Harsh words then on your tongue, in my mouth
only sounds that stumbled forward
for the border guards, their hands
hard and fast for contraband.

Later, I stand outside your door,
listening to your breath come slow
between the shutters, wondering who
would be left to regret us.
Your one letter months from then,
breathless with dashes and wide-open
vowels—the letter I never answered
for fear you'd follow it
or understand the wanderer's cowardice
that filled my body
with your name.

                    "Next year
I'll be gone," you said.
  "London, Santiago, New York . . ."
You slapped your hands in that strange
Brasilian gesture: *"Não se não"*—

Who knows? I ask now,
twenty years since corpses floated
under the Mapocho River bridges,
and the rich women of Santiago
parked their cars along the bank
to stare at the dark-skinned ones
among them, and all letters out of Chile
stopped. Twenty years since Marisa
lay down with the child whose name
never reached us, since Chico
slept with a revolver by his pillow
and Marcos finally won his game
of Russian roulette.

Twenty years,
Wander Luís, since you sat cross-legged
on a curbstone in the only photo
I have of you, in a white shirt
with its pocketsful of cigarettes
and ballpoints, strumming a *frêvo* rhythm
on your dead brother's guitar,
your eyes half-closed, your face,
like his, never getting any older.

The Opening Up, 1972

That was the year Caetano Veloso
returned a hero to Bahia,
his hair shaved in the prison
grown long again, his songs
full of exile's English
driving the *samba*-school dancers wild.

Who remembers the old tunes
hidden behind the years?
Brasil, 1500: dull flush of torches
over the wharves at Santos, slaveships
with crosses burned into their sails
hove in for the midnight docking.
The triangle trade.
Those who survived the crossing
sold away from their true names,
stumbling chained onto the gangplanks.

Now slums of Pernambuco
roll away the same stone,
men in dress uniforms and jackboots
on the balcony of the presidential villa
sign their shadows into law . . .

and Caetano steps off the Varig jet,
his face haggard with British winter.
We look at his new lyrics,
photos we've clipped from magazines—
Caetano on the cover of *Manchete*,
Veja, in some Ipanema beach house,
splashing in the pool with Gal
and Gil and Maria Bethânia,
flashing his good-luck smile.

He'd learned his lesson,
blunting the untempered
metal of his voice, saying
Never again get your hopes up.
As crowds swarm the sound truck
to touch him, he sings "White Wing,"
"Rain, Sweat, and Beer"—*Asa branca, Chuva
suor e cerveja.* He sings *Things
are getting better better better better
Bethânia* to the lovely sons
and daughters of mixed blood,
Dorival in prison a hundred years
back in the brain, crying
I promise you my darling I'll return.

La Push

for David Heineck

We started late, hitched past lumber camps
that drowsed in hemlock shadow
on Highway 101—towns with names
like Sappho, Forks—down the one-lane
spur road to the Bogachiel Crossing,
river rapids pounding rocks
into a rounded hum.

The coastal burn—lodgepole pines
leaned over whitewater with fire-
slashed crowns. Our ride an empty
logging rig with one flatbed
shelved upon the other, roaring
through alder and sumac thickets

where the roadway rippled with heat
between bald slopes of the clear cut.
Cedar shade a cool blur
at the reservation's edge,
we rolled across the plank bridge
into La Push. The coast.

We thanked the driver and jumped out,
flat of my hand steadied a moment
on the cab's exhaust stack
and I heard my own scream like someone else's
as the shock burned through: my hand seared
like the skin of survivors
stumbling from a fire
no one was meant to get away from.

I collapsed in cedar needles
at the road's edge.
You tore your old shirt
for bandages, we made our way
on the gravel track through town

between battered pickups and jalopies
up on blocks, bait shacks and the long sedans
of tourists from Seattle come to fish.

The first aid station
we could find—a red cross
riddled with BB shot, a trailer
sunken among windfall hemlock
where a girl with bruise-shadowed eyes
sold us ointment and one
gauze patch, and glared
when we asked about a doctor.

We followed our own footprints out,
the only visitors from the city
not armored in our cars.
Jagged wind off the seastacks
cut through me, my skin
tattered linen in a firestorm,
your body arching over mine—
nowhere to crumple into safety
or that true homeland, sleep.

Quillayute fishermen on the listing pier
paused from hauling in their nets.
They watched us, their eyes
the forest-slashing fall of pines.
We knew only the salt weight
of wind, shallow network of roots
in our syllables, the ancestors'
exhausted names.

                    Nothing for you here,
the eyes said,
the closed doors of the shadows.

Afternoon passed a roughened hand
over the sun's eye, spirits of cedars
leaning against gaunt cliffs.
We turned away from shadows.

Whatever we might have wished
mere signals that went up in smoke,
exhaust of a homebound fisherman's
late-model van. The lift he gave us
through fire-scored salmonberry
and Oregon grape: singe-marks

inevitable as skin and its many obligations.
He drove us back to the state's
resurfaced road and on to a clinic
in Hoquiam, and waved away the crumpled
bills we offered for gas fare.

At evening's sidereal frontier, the sun
slipped into the undivided sea.

Aymara Woman on Socabaya Street

(Potosí, Bolivia)

She squats on the corner,
a cud of *coca* wadded in one cheek.
Whatever the inside of a stone thinks
must shine in her
as she spins a spool of wool
in and out of her fingers,
the center in a wheel of skirts.
Onions in baskets and bowls
filled with corn gruel at her feet.
Shrug of her shawl to ward off my eye
and she's faceless. A padded
alpaca hump.

Faint bulbs strung in a mine
glow on hands sorting
over the moving belts.
Fingers blink across the tin.
Bulbs swing as a rumble
dawns deep in the rock.
The glow on fingers stutters
as the roof falls in, dark
as shawls pitched over the sun.

She speaks to me
in a tongue guttural as lead.
A creased hand paws my pocket.
I gesture, I have nothing.
Her eyes flint hard against mine,
she spits out her name for me
with a curse and laughs.
What she invokes
turns the corner with me.

That night, my dreams
file like miners from their shafts,
carrying the old words
knotted in *sisal*, gold masks
from faces with no memories.
In abandoned cities,
five-hundred-year-old echoes
catch up to their cries.
Over the high ranges,
axes go up and down.
Strange hands loosen on the stone.

Eugenia

"Arauco tiene una pena
que no la puedo callar."
—Violeta Parra

Where are you now, Eugenia?
Are you still climbing
the rain-scarred road out of Arauco?
You're eleven, carrying water
—two cutaway tin buckets
with baling-wire handles—
your head lowered, black hair cropped,
a child of brave words
and shoulders broadened by homespun.

I still see you standing
against the cinder-block wall
of the Save the Children Fund office,
do you remember?
You clutch your printed number card,
trying to make the right face
for the rich ladies,
flicker of disbelief in your eyes
as the shutter-gun flashes, your name
tumbling into hundreds of mailboxes
at the end of the month.

On the Arauco Road, you're yourself
again. At your door, chickens
dart in and out across the lintel.
Your grandmother between bean rows
shields her eyes from the watery sun
of the coastland. Mother-of-pearl woman
under a spun-wool sky, gray braids
roped together down her back,
smoke from the cooking fire
on the packed earth floor
working its way through her shadow.

Eleven more years will pass
after you ask me in for supper.
After I watch you hurry back
and forth for kindling and *mate* leaves
as evening takes over the one small window
and I finally catch on: tonight
there are no beans, no bread, no *mate*.

The next day, I sign up for you,
bring apples and cheese
because today's your birthday.
My friends and I take you to Café Lebu
where the Peace Corps eats.
You sit wordless, shy,
concentrating on your hamburger
and homefries and the *gauchos* in hats
and spurs galloping around borders
of the placemats. You nod yes
to every question, try not to stare
at what we leave on our plates.

Madriña, godmother, you call me
in the seven years of letters
—those construction-paper cards
listing sweaters and shoes and medicines—
and a snapshot of you every Christmas.
Your hair in ribbons, longer now,
arms around schoolbooks or gifts
my money buys.
                        Each year
you're taller, almost a woman,
but your writing never changes—
the same blue copybook scrawl
and the same question:
When would I return?

I never did, Eugenia, and at eighteen
your letters stopped.
                        Was there a man—
some dark-mantled farmer who rode past you
on his way to town—mustachioed,
lashing his pony, and you whispered

Arbolé, arbolé, seco y verdé,
a song you'd memorized in school,
as he waved? Did you go
with some miner's son
who drove his oxcart for you
from the bituminous smoke of Lota?
Do your own lungs blacken
as you wait with the other women
in the ration lines at dawn?

Or were you among those rounded up
in the Coronel strikes, rumors
of *desaparecidos* at the Dawson Island camp,
their names lost and found
and lost again in the headlines?

How do you live, Eugenia?
There is no one I can speak to.
My letters come back unopened,
a 3 x 5 blank in the file
where your picture was.

Have you followed what Violeta Parra
cried for, chanting Arauco's sorrow
that nobody could silence?
Are you still waiting in the rain
and glacial distance for the long train
from the North? In this undecided season,
it's time I came back
as I promised, when you pressed
the *copihue* blooms into my hands,
the national flower of your hunger.

The Grade School Teacher During Recess

(Jamaica Plain, Boston)

She falls back, shuffling
the spelling tests. Fifteen minutes
to stare at cardboard lions
in the wall zoo, take out
the confiscated slingshots.
Write a letter to a lover
doing time for grief. Other days

she stands guard on the playground.
Big boys bully the ball, girls
drop their hopscotch counters
and dance across the chalk lines
toward the boys. At age nine
the adults already emerging
from their faces. Every schoolday

they slam the desks down, carefully
forgetting their homework.
They go back to pork 'n' beans
and pasteboard-covered windows.
In the guerrilla theatre
of the way it is, they've known
their lines for years.

The teacher folds the letter
under the Batman comic strip,
takes out the long division, waiting
for the class to shove its way
into the room. She puts back on
the authoritarian's eyebrows,
the quiet child who stays in
from recess to read ahead
already disappearing from her face.

For Elizabeth Ríos

Victor Jara (1932–1973)

*"Son años pasados, presentes en mí,
Era ya en Santiago, y te conocí ..."*
          —Isabel Parra

So I'm here again, five feet away
from you, on the makeshift stage
of the Peña de los Parra,
and you're singing *The Right to Live
in Peace*, still in your actor's
leather jacket, embracing your shadow
in the guitar, the darkened room
taking its shape around you.
You tell us of Camilo Torres
and of Amanda—the young woman
who ran through your town's wet streets
to meet her lover, and found him
gunned down at the factory gate.

What do you think of us, students
hunching forward to listen
in the smoky light, glasses
of *vino tinto* beside us, the room
deep and wine-colored, Allende's photo
behind you on the wall?
We follow your lead,
singing the choruses over and over.
We stand when you do, chanting
Otra! Otra! till you play another,
the fields of Chile in your voice,
your guitar speaking its human song.

I never talk to you then.
I'm shy as rain in your country,
the language too much yours.
You stand between sets
in the crowded patio, one
among many, those who sing
La Nueva Canción. You're not even
one of my favorites.

Did you know then that shadows
would swallow the back galleries
like memories no one could get used to?
That you'd sleep in shifts
those last days, taking your turns
at the locked gate, the shortwave
radio crackling with surveillance?

You'd refuse the last chance
to destroy the tapes, your songs
filled with those who did
what they had to, lined up against walls
of the Estadio Nacional.
How could you believe it
when the time came, and your voice
grew too big for the cell
where they broke your hands
because they couldn't make you stop?

Once again it's September,
and I sit in this small kitchen
listening to Isabel Parra sing
Como una historia, her lament
for your death. Her voice breaks
in the tape, telling the names
that make nothing easier, our words
that cannot reach you, foghorns
sounding all night on the river
like a story from someone else's life.

Survivor's Story

For Istvan

A high wind blows across your life,
how you fled with your parents
all night through Hungary's
hills and fields: 1956,
the October Revolution,
a book hero's adventure for you
between the searchlights and flares,
crawling into the West under pasture wire
as tanks rolled through your village's
one main street, and Soviet troops
stormed house after house for survivors.

In school, Vienna,
you were a rift in the regime,
the strange language piling up
in your sentences. Your parents' words
wore yellow stars for flight.
Rucksacks packed and ready
in the closets, Passover's bitter herbs
and flatbread—reminders nailed in
at every family gathering.
There was nowhere you weren't a stranger.

Later, in America, your father
finally talked about the *Anschluss*.
Loudspeakers over the shunting yards
after the mass arrests, families
standing all night between machine-gun towers,
trainloads of those who would vanish.
Camp numbers burned
into your father's arms,
your mother in Budapest
sealed behind the flimsy hope
of a doorway.

                     Their warnings
in what remained of your boyhood
almost your own—numbers so final
they left traces in the veins,
children who could never walk
into a darkened room alone.
You mastered the conflicting syllables
of the major powers, concealed
your hesitation at the door.
Teachers gave you gold stars
for the story's faultless grammar.

Where, within this scattered inheritance
did you acquire your joy?
Not from the dropping away
of extra names, the everyday face
you put on for your daughters,
your wife for whom everything
must be lived again.

Not from the all-night intercoms
of clinics, operating rooms floodlit
like that other theater, war.
The homeland of your listening.
Wards where those who survived long past themselves
whisper their stories in languages
the dead can't help them to forget.

Moment by moment, you must forgive,
you say, the star that crossed your past
with such fatal scintillation,
give love its safe-conduct.
                          Then you understand
why wind speaks its high mind
in your blood, why physicians
need not justify the healer's vigil
when they lie awake, counting boxcars
on the first trains from the front.

(Ollantaitambo, Perú)

I stepped off the Cuzco–Machu
Picchu local, and the thin air
reeled with constellations.
I asked the way to town.
The station master swung his oil lamp
and our smudged faces
flickered on its panes.

No, he didn't know the roads,
the platform's widening rings
of dark. He never held in mind
what dropped away over the edges
of a city woman's sight.
"But this *cholita*"—he pointed
to a shape bent under bundles
and layers of shawls—"can take you.
They all know the way."

The woman assented in a warble
high and strange as a candle
flickering in a mountain shrine.
She turned and walked.
I took my pack and followed.

The Inca woman trudged ahead
on the rutted *llama* track,
her silence dark and tightly braided.
Above us, eucalyptus limbs
held up the night.

Other shapes fell in behind,
stocky and silent as my guide.
I shifted the pack's unbalanced load,
shrank into layers of my own dark.
Among forms that fit the path
—like priests in whatever road
their god guides them—I had to save
myself from stumbling.

Oil lamps in windows
fixed our silhouettes. The road
turned into town. In the square
the crowd disbanded, lamps
went down like lids.
The Inca woman moved up the mountain
to her hut of fitted stone.

I moved alone through the streets,
speechless, dark as faces
extinguished under shawls,
trying to empty myself of all names
and summon the courage
to knock on windowless plank doors
and ask the blank-faced dwellers for a room.

The Retarded Woman on Cooper Street

(Missoula, Montana)

Every day, the man next door
locks his wife out in the yard.
Under August's tattered cottonwoods
she talks back to steel guitar chords
that slide out of loudspeakers
strapped to the cyclone fence—
a slurred contralto, lyric
from the Love Generation
already twenty revolutions gone
under a sun that will never be younger.

The woman flails at a nimbus of bottle flies
circling the six-pack of Orange Crush
he's left her. She can't finish one
before she's opening another,
like a child left to herself
with a cookie jar. She laughs
at Hmong women on their knees
between pepper plants next yard over.
She calls them names from a war
in which no one could have saved her.

At five, her husband unbolts the gate,
hands her his Green Beret lunchbox.
It falls open in the unclaimed space
between them. Already we begin to suspect
his attention span. She stoops
to pick up sandwich bags.
There are plum bruises where
her stretch slacks ride up her calves.

What do others know
of self-damage and its lockouts?
They move between plastic marigolds
up the dirt path to the porch.
She glances back, her face
pockmarked with questions.

"Get going, move!" he gestures,
voice drowned by Great Northern whistles
from shunting yards along the river.
They go in. The screen door
slams soundlessly behind them.

Next door, Hmong girls
wrapped in bright appliqué *ao dais*
like memories of river willows
exploding into monsoon flower.
They gaze across rows of leeks
and Chinese cabbage at a lawn
littered as truce in a DMZ.

Their faces blurred in smoke
from the freight yard's iron couplings,
they have no words yet in our tongue
for all that has happened,
loudspeakers on the fence
still blaring a song that said
all the right things once,
that has long since made its money.

The year Salvador Allende died
she and I walked unlit paths
of the park along the river,
the only women in Santiago
who stayed out all night.
At the bridge she stopped.
"*Gringa*, I'm sick and tired
of this town."
                        Born in Hiroshima
seven years after the Bomb,
she had no time for fools.
Her mother arranged cut stems
before the lacquered screens,
her father the only karate teacher
in the city. Their apartment staked out
with azaleas and concealed alarms.

She worked late at the Art School,
took busses to shacktowns by the river
to hand out packets of dried milk
to the women. Weekends, she waited
by the stage of the Peña de los Parra
for Horacio's second set to finish,
playing along, tuning her *charango*
down to his, watching his hands
on the fast bars.
                        She was the one
they talked about, the one in poncho
with crow's-wing hair, practicing
an Andean cane flute between classes.
Bolivian, they said, to avoid
their real thoughts.

At Horacio's house across the river
we watched Allende's speeches on TV,
and I asked the wrong question.
Horacio turned on me: "You don't know
anything about the Revolution."

She took me to meetings
where we learned the new means of production
and someone snapped pictures—a roomful
of students with straight black hair
and armbands the color of the flag.
She called me *sister*, and I almost
convinced myself I belonged.

That night, she left my party early.
I glimpsed her hours later
from my window—walking alone, head down,
guitar slung over one shoulder,
her shadow under the street lamp
belonging to no one.
Along the river, walls
were covered with slogans by morning.

She wrote me when I left.
"Horacio's gone, I'm living with
a Cuban now, it won't be long
before we bring two roads together."
That was late August, 1973,
and I waited all season for her news.

September, they carried Allende
out of the gutted capitol.
The darkened trains ran all night,
the ground hardly daring to shudder.
Her parents looked at each other
over photos whose outlines they traced
like Braille in their sleep.

What about letters that never arrived,
silence at the other end
of the telegraph? The city
of doorbells no one answered,
lights out in houses where shadows had no
permission to show themselves?

Will I ever know her story.
I ask myself what I'd give
for the forbidden speeches to be wound again
onto the brain's spool, the photographs
to fall back into the ransacked drawers.
For hastily painted words to realign
like bones along the flooded river.

She was the only one who ever
called me what I could have been—
someone whose name fades from my book
of lost addresses. My hand that
forgets itself and writes.

Post-Revolutionary Letter

After cities full of flashbacks and bad debts,
you send me a letter from a country
safely out of reach,
your get-even scorecard: Love
or nothing.
              Should I wish myself
into your place? You rented a room
above the gun-runners' bar,
fumes of *chicha* and kerosene
through floorboards, men in shirtsleeves
hunched over tables in a low room,
their tongues loosened by Molotov cocktails
and the jokes you could be shot
on sight for telling.

You shuffled a stacked deck,
spent hours dialing area codes
of fallen countries, friends
who disappeared in unmarked cars
before dawn. You say you want me again
but everything has its price.

                  Memory lapses,
hands losing their nerve, fingers
pointing to the *Keep Out* signs,
telling us whom to hate.
Were you always in the vanguard,
with a cause you could get strangers
to believe in? Did you wonder
how you got there, when fireworks
strafed the night sky, and amputees
from the last war crawled under benches?

In the duty-free shops, vodka
dropped like mercury in the bottles.
Rifles filled the crates marked *Shoes*,
and bribed inspectors whistled,
looking out across winter hills.

The years are worn out
by forwarding addresses, everything I said
twisted by your dictum—*Don't Look Back*.
I put your letter down.
I won't be at the airport
listening to doctored radio reports
and making out with the taxi driver
till you arrive.

Coplas for Violeta Parra (1917–1967)

> *"Tu dolor es un círculo infinito*
> *Que no comienza ni termina nunca ..."*
> —Nicanor Parra

How could we have known you, Violeta?
You were spirit-flower, honeycomb, long
shadow of a circle-dance by the time
we leaned against *café* tables in the smoky
crepuscule of the Peña de los Parra

and your daughter Isabel sang
Gracias a la vida, "Thanks to Life,"
the room full of listeners flushed
with homemade wine and the hours your last song's
joy and sorrow ached inside you.

Song that pushed us into memory's
long dissolve: winter 1954,
woman with a voice like Temuco rain
and a face no one had written on
stepped from Pablo's house at Isla Negra

under ship's-prow mermaids and the salt-
indicted flag of Chile. Cradling your *charango*
like the body of a child, you strummed
the *cueca, sirilla*—dances from which
no one could free us. Who was with you

at the all-night wakes? You sang *a lo divino*
to the dead child, *a lo humano* to survivors
who swayed with their grief till dawn
freed them from its waltz-grip, radiant
darkness blooming from the singer.

You trudged the cattle-saddened tracks under
Ñuble's cloud cover, and staggered on
the drenched deck of the woodcutter's scow
as it bucked storm swells in riptide's channels
off Chiloé. *Según el favor del viento.*

As per the favor of the wind, you
navigated whole vortices of storm,
soft coal discoloring in the hold.
St. Elmo's fire in the crossbeams,
you called down the sinner's clarion.

Sepia-toned photos pin you to gone
moments, woman in a peasant sweater
hunched at a table in the *ruca*
of Pitrufquén, dipping bread into goat's
broth, reading your handcuffed brother's letters.

You heard him rattle the window grate
at dawn, fists beat blistered walls of the cell.
His voice rang out between blows—*décimas*
encoded the distance between you,
ten syllables per line of your lament.

Blurred tones of older histories—you sat
in the doorway, spinning tapestries
from hand-dyed wool the way the hermit
thrush couldn't help herself for singing.
Arpilleras: networks of birds in dream-

embroidered branches. Guitars inlaid
with mother-of-pearl leaned against walls
like inquisitor's examples, a harp
stood upright in the corner, a mortal
witness. Why did you throw yourself away?

That winter, you pounded a *cultrún*
in a shamaness's trance, chanting
Arauco's sorrow. Paris: Chants du Monde,
your voice lost for years in a desk drawer
between the revolution and the coup.

What drove you north on the ore trains to
the Atacama: high desert decades
without rain, the sun white phosphorus
in sky *like a hell without a door*?
Alberto: twenty years between you

like the Bío-Bío in flood spate. River
of division: no unconquered warchief
stepped from the sky-tomb of Caupolicán
and strode through the *conquistadores'*
fusillade. Alberto's gaunt face always

in profile, bloodlust and melancholy
hunched over the arterial throb
of the horsehide drum. The man whose grief-
struck measures were your own. Whose life always
would be elsewhere, between too early

and too late, what-if's and that's-the-breaks,
condolences and love in vain. That night
you went to him naked, offering
yourself, and he in his confusion
told the truth.

                    Could you have healed yourself
those last hours, the full moon stricken
through torn flaps of the carnival tent
outside the village, where you let midnight
leave the sky without you? You went back

to age seventeen, you were ivy
ramifying on the lattice, only
love's science stripped of consolation
returned you pure and simple to yourself.
In the mind's arc, the three-dimensional

erasure of breath, one pistol shot
and its concentric echoes, you laid
your head on your guitar, woman whose grief
was meted out, ten syllables per line,
whose children took no other name but yours.

"Arbeit Macht Frei"
            —motto over the entrance of every
            Nazi concentration camp

We walk in under the empty tower, snow
falling on barbed-wire nets where the bodies
of suicides hung for days. We follow signs
to the treeless square, where the scythe blade, hunger,
had its orders, and some lasted hours in the cold
when all-night roll calls were as long as winter.

We've come here deliberately in winter,
field stubble black against the glare of snow.
Our faces go colorless in wind, cold
the final sentence of their bodies
whose only identity by then was hunger.
The old gate with its hated grillework sign

walled off, we take snapshots to sign
and send home, to show we've done right by winter.
We've eaten nothing, to stand inside their hunger.
We count, recount crimes committed in snow—
those who sheltered their dying fellows' bodies
from the work details, the transport trains, the cold.

Before the afternoon is gone, the cold
goes deep, troops into surrendered land. Signs
direct us to one final site, where bodies
slid into brick-kiln furnaces all winter
or piled on iron stretchers in the snow
like a plague year's random harvest. What hunger

can we claim? Those who had no rest from hunger
stepped into the ovens, knowing already the cold
at the heart of the flame. They made no peace with snow.
For them no quiet midnight sign
from on high—what pilgrims seek at the bottom of winter—
only the ebbing measure of their lives. Their bodies

are shadows now, ashing the footprints of everybody
who walks here, ciphers carrying the place of hunger
for us, who journey so easily in winter.
Who is made free by the merciless work of cold?
What we repeat when we can't read the signs—
the story of our own tracks breaking off in snow.

Snow has covered the final account of their bodies
but we must learn the signs: they hungered,
they were cold, and in Dachau it was always winter.

The Hammerer

(Provincetown, Cape Cod)

Every night at eleven
the one-armed sculptor
starts hammering in his studio
at the far end of the building.

The painter listens for shapes
she's glimpsed through his window
to assemble: the sheet-metal
Pietà, sand-cast dragons rising
from a map of the Mekong Delta.

Lights go out across the way
as if in disapproval.
Upstairs, the painter puts on chowder
for the fifth night,
mixes pigments in the broken sink
while the saucepan blackens,
skylights above her glaze over
with a steam patina: condensation
with no power to deflect the dark.

She closes the stove's eye
and the hammering stops,
as if he forgot himself,
tried to shift the hammer
to his other hand.
She rereads her dead husband's letters
as she eats, absentmindedly puts back
bones she fished out of the chowder.

The hammerer goes at it again.

She thinks of her husband slumped
over the twisted wheel of a jeep
while mortars flared, flash fires
guttered out in a barrage of green,

monsoon's nightmare underside
in the minefield of his brain.
Another woman's bloodstained letters
fell from his pocket
when they pulled him out.

In the hammerer's studio
she pictures a decibel sculpture,
white as a child's cry
in an abandoned building.
A street closed off where a car
careened through plate glass
and the evening news exploded into flame.

How else, the painter asks herself,
to fight fire? She wants each blow
of iron on stone, each arc
of the welder's torch
to burn deeper into the brain's
will to remember, the magic circle
she draws around herself
and all that has happened.

At midnight, pounding and a neighbor's angry voice
storm the hammerer's white cubicle
of noise. Colors swirl in the painter's jars
like unresolved conversations.
As if lovers' thoughts linger
in passageways, and she goes on reading letters
of a man with an unforgiven life.

At the building's far end
studio lights snap off.
In the long let-down of silence
she washes and puts away the plates,
remembers calls she tried to make each night
when no operator could have placed
a cry for assistance.

She lets herself out the front door
and starts down the ship's-plank verandah
to the sculptor's studio.

                                    Beyond
his window's squares of light,
sand with nothing but sand beneath it
shifts enormous hills before the wind
and bare trees like nervous systems
hold up the night.

The Room

For Margaret Gibson, R.N.

She stood in the room where Allende died.
It was two months later,
Armistice Day, 1973,
and she was on a package tour
for which all refunds had been cancelled.
Below the bombed-out windows
with their twisted grillework,
Pinochet's troops patrolled the streets,
and she wore a scarlet poppy
for that other war—Flanders Field
and the black-edged telegram
that had stopped her father's face
in its frame on the mantelpiece.

For years she would not tell this story:
how she walked through Santiago's
rubble-strewn streets until soldiers
leaped from a van with naked bayonets
and surrounded her, ripping her camera
from her shoulder. All afternoon in the *cuartel*
she showed them blurry Polaroids
of palm trees and big hotels,
and told them she knew nothing.
She wasn't working for anyone.
As late sun slanted through the one window's
iron bars, the *comandante* suddenly
relented. "We have something special
to show you." His tone said
You'd better not refuse.

A guard led her through cratered beds
and shattered statuary of the garden,
into the high-ceilinged room
already beginning to fill with twilight.

Everything was as they had left it.
She gazed a long time
at the red plush chair,
the heavy desk with bullet marks,
scorched books piled knee-deep
on the floor.
                   "Communist books,"
the guard said, shifting
the rifle on his shoulder.
There was a battered telephone
on the desktop, and a letter
handwritten in Spanish,
the fountain pen lying across it
where the words trailed off.

She knew no Spanish.
The guard stepped to the window.
She wanted to take the letter
or engrave it in her thoughts
for her friends outside, but the guard
turned back and there was no way
she could go beyond this warning.
She studied the prescription bottle
by the inkwell: nitroglycerin
he took for his congested heart.
On the floor under the sideboard
a whiskey bottle on its side, cracked open,
a spill of dark residue beside it.
"*El Presidente* liked his booze,"
the guard smirked, as if
that justified everything.

Her eyes had been saving the blood
for last. In the failing light
the dark stains stood out black—
his last call to his wife,
his farewell to Chile on the radio
when he knew they were coming for him.

Spatter on the walls still echoing
the burst door, the rifle barrels
raised, automatic fire going on and on.
Vanishing in shadow the pool
of himself into which he fell.

Outside, wail of the curfew sirens,
footsteps of those who could be shot
on sight for delaying. "Don't worry,
we escort you back," the guard said.
"We know how to treat our friends."

For years she would feel the click
of the safety catch, chill of steel
at her temple, the poppy's crimson
deepening on her breast.
She said *No thank you*
and walked out.
If soldiers tried to stop her
she would turn and face them
as she still wanted to believe
he had.

The Peace Corps Volunteer Comes Home

Carrying the Kodak prints
she sent, her parents meet her
at the depot: What has she made
of the Third World?

The answer comes to her
like marked money—Brasil's
old joke: "*Café e Pelé*."
The principal exports.
She doesn't mention the color
of her lover's hands.

Her mother wrote, "Bring home
the coffee, nothing but the coffee."
She's a big girl now, she brings home
the rhythm, *Orfeo Negro*
in her walk. Her gray eyes
darkening in equatorial light.

At the Steak 'n' Ale, *feijoada*
lingers on her tongue. She waves away
the New York cut. Recife, she says,
Safety Zone. Good roads, and machetes
working through the cane.

                                    Father nods,
turns off the burglar alarms
in his thoughts. Mother brings out
the china pattern, shows
what she's added.

Neither wants to know their daughter
sleeps in the other world, dreams
in the passion flower's language,
balancing the unbroken promise
of a man's body
against her, carrying the love child,
silence, like a *figa* charm.

Message to César Vallejo

Caught in the crosswind
of my desires, I'm here
to stay: New Orleans,
Crescent City along the river
that still moves underground
to take the dead in its arms.
Where moss creeps down
ropes on the hanging trees,
and the children of mixed blood
carefully whiten the faces
in the photo albums. I hear
the blues through a grillework door:
I can't go on this way.

Vallejo, you would understand
how a lover's memory of home
opens the shuttered windows,
and know why he still paces off
outlines of the auction block.
How we don't owe any explanation
for where we don't belong.

I read your exile's life again.
Those months in the Chicama Valley
you watched Indians come back at dusk
from the sugarfields for the day's
handful of rice, the sweat of alcohol
on credit, your first poems
burning the plantation storehouse
to the ground. Trujillo's jail
and España falling on its thorns.
Even then you knew
how border towns are everywhere
and the passport that opens them
a switchblade through melons.

No more excuses, you would say.
No listening for the lover's key
in the lock, breath like mosquito netting
I've wrapped myself in.
Suitcases are too easy,
the army blanket from Da Nang
at the foot of the bed
another reason not to stay.

You never went home to Huamachuco.
What you knew Good Friday,
1938, crying those last words
from your bed: *"I want to go
to Spain!"* as Franco's troops
swept down the Ebro Valley to the sea.

César, I'm staying.
I, whose people starved
during the York enclosures
and burned at the stake
in Zürich, know how often my name
was written in the logbooks
of slaveships. I cancel
the exit visas I thought
my life depended on.

Josie Bliss, October 1971

*"Nombre definitivo que cae en las semanas
con un golpe de acero que las mata."*
—Pablo Neruda, *Residencia en la tierra*

When they brought me the newspaper
headlines with your name translated
to the round dark petals of our script,
I knew you'd finally found your love.
I'm happy for you, Pablo.
After all these years, silence
between us like seabottom jewels,
the Bay of Bengal with jellyfish armadas
patrolling the beachheads from which
I could wage no campaign against loss,
your face in the photo
grown heavier—faithful, at last,
to the body's vows with earth.
Our season of mangoes and brainfire,
the paraffin lamp guttering out
on the other side of the curtain,
white jasmines in my hair
and naked feet you said you loved.
Forget those foolish nights
I circled the bed with a knife,
a dance the old women showed me—
panther's ritual, incense I burned
to weaken your instinct for betrayal.
I was your first love,
wasn't I? No spell
bound with camphor and inflections
missing for thousands of years
in our mouths can change that.
Remember how I said my fears
would end with your death?
When you gave death the slip,
boarding the westbound freighter,
leaving your freshly ironed shirts
to fend for themselves, and books
like a row of hostile witnesses,

in languages you returned to
every morning, every night you cried out
in your sleep—it was I
who died: into the betel leaf
and fringed anxiety of palm,
sarongs and Malay silks stacked
like jute bales in the courtyard.
Airless nights and the ache of salt
between my thighs, my body closed up
like a village in wartime.
No steamer passage across an ocean
littered with telegrams and the summons
of fair-skinned women, no hampers
of saffron rice and clear plum wine
to remind you, no conjures of sweet oil
and scimitars could break the spell of flesh
to which I lost you.
You wouldn't recognize me now,
Pablo. I've blurred with age
and sons and the long war in the East.
And the one daughter they took from me,
whose secret name meant Heartbreak
in our tongue, and in your language,
Song. Veiled in blue silk for the voyage,
she vanished from the docks at Singapore
into abject air, water the color
of a beating. Now I'm alone,
refugee of the blood's terrain,
memory's backhanded apologists.
No husband to uproot the strangle-vine,
no one to put a stop
to these voices—my share of messages
you could never bring yourself
to send. What else remains
of what we called our lives?
The house with the jagged bamboo fence
went back to the tribe of liana
and baobab and climbing fern.
My brothers in their blood-colored pagodas
came for me, snake bracelets on their arms,
their tongues heavy as bronze
bell clappers. In Mandalay market

they sold my true name—a powder
against suspicion and English ways.
Since then I am married to quarry stone
and razor-palm green air,
desire that honeycombs the brain
like limewater, fool's-gold gleam
in passageways of no return.
Gone the parrot's emerald laugh,
the incantations of monkey flower
you used against the shadows. Gone
the history of broken clay you told,
gone the hard fruit wrapped in *tilak* skin
that began our countries' sad,
metallic generations. Gone your tongue
in my mouth, sweet anarchy of the hands.
Don't look for me, Pablo,
if you come. I am the first wife
and widow of my own refusals.
In this neighborhood of narrow doors
and shadow longings, the retreating steps
of my blue daughter, machine-gun
voices of my sons, I have forgotten
how to open dawn's orange fan.
No more do I search through books
full of dreams' high-water marks,
no more glide from room to room
listening to your pale breath,
my own lost pulse along the heartwire.
No more do I throw myself down
and kiss the chalk feet of the bearded god.
Stay in your land of stone's tremor
and women like the avalanche's blessing.
I couldn't bear the hidden fault lines
in your beauty, and I no longer answer
to the empty net, the long-knived
moon—warnings between the hand
and its caressing, names you gave
me for my fury and my joy.

II
Flowers in Winter

"Who has bid thee ask no more
How fares my life? To play the enemy
And ask not where he dwells
Who was thy friend?"

—Hafiz of Shiraz

Flowers in Winter

I

I sit alone now among the lyrebirds,
the twining rose and jasmine of this garden,
woven image of the bower, you said,
where the poet's lost friend dwells.

Isfahan: pure silk, a thousand knots
in a hand's breadth, and a peacock-tail shimmer
when I lift it to the window's
changing light.

　　　　　　Flowers in winter
we called your gift, profusion of the senses
I fought against, those first days
when the season burrowed into my lungs
and there was scarcely a language between us.

II

In the breakfast room of a Nürnberg hotel
you were another dark-haired man
in Europe on some unguessable errand,

and I a woman with too many books
who never stayed more than three days
in one city, who locked her door
before sleep and nursed her cough
all night, like a lover.

"If I don't hear that cough again,"
you said in your tentative English,
"I think maybe I am something lost."
Three days passed while we talked
before we thought to ask each other's names.

III

It wasn't your hand on my arm
under the station's broken clock face
that persuaded me to stay,
or the cities closed in upon themselves
at the year's end, or my woman's fear
of being once again a stranger.

We stood at your window that night
and drained the old year from our glasses.
In the flush of French liqueur,
and stroboscopic flowerings of fireworks

—as if above the floodlit ruins
the Allied squadrons had returned—

could we forget there was a war on,
there were many wars, our nations
declared or undeclared in all of them?

Could we forget the afternoon we climbed
the fortress tower's thousand steps
for a view of what was left
of the Führer's favorite city?
Photos of the bomb-gutted neighborhoods
on every corner, and the words beneath—

"Nürnberg, 1945: *Nie wieder*."
Never again.

We spent hours in the café
on Albrecht Dürerplatz, watching snow
deepen on the Gothic cobblestones,
half-timbered gables of the few houses
that survived,

while you recited poets
who flourished in your tongue
—Rumi, Saadi, and Khayyam.
You improvised your translations
into German—a Northern forest
where you'd learned to make your way,
crossed iron staves of its syllables
taking on sunlight and the floral
intertwinings of your script.

How could I answer you?
I'd been taught to suspect men
who spoke no language I was easy with.
In me they would see only what static-
ravaged screens in steamy theatres hinted.
I had not begun to override
the voice of my own deluded girlhood—

This one's not like all the others.

We are all too much like the others.
I watched your face
as I repeated it.

I was afraid of my willingness to learn,
to let this smoke-darkened speech
that belonged to neither of us
deepen its hold: the only country
where two outsiders would be free to meet,
while armed guards beyond the borders
went on changing their formations.

I knew too much already
to pretend I didn't understand
the ancient word in Persian
for Beloved: *Friend.*

IV

For days I tried
and gave up trying to move on,
to lose you in Salzburg,
Venice, or Trieste,
knowing whatever I did
was neither right nor wrong,
that the rules turned their heads
and no one else could decide for us.

You were merely a small man
with lovely eyes and a gift for languages,
from a village in Azerbaijan
where you had to make it on your own
after the ayatollahs emptied the Throne
of Thrones, and all the schools
you were named for closed.

"It's too late for me,"
you said. "I grew up waiting
for busses that didn't come,
where all who said so much as
                        The sky
is getting darker
                              to a stranger
were dragged away into a darkness
that closed the sky forever."

You did what you could
with what remained,
shipping your wares from provinces
where the finest artisans were proud
of how the knot patterns they'd gotten by heart
went dim.
                  Their minds, you said, full
of Allah's light and the shadows
of unbelievers beyond their looms,
blindness a high honor
in a land where the most advanced degree
was survival.

V

                                 I didn't believe
I was your first lover.
The night you finally begged me
out of my clothes
there was too much wisdom in your hands
and your tongue knew exactly
where to find me. In spite of myself
I wanted only to fold up my plans
and follow where you moved inside me.

VI

Where could we go from there?
In the empty second-class car
through obliterated fields, too absorbed
in each other's thoughts to speak,
each in our different languages.

In the oblique light of the Hanseatic ports
I was the woman whose presence
remained unexplained,
while well-dressed men on their knees
peeled carpets from the showroom stack
and heaped them with the dusty thud
of merchandise at your feet.

I sat by myself,
staring out plate-glass windows
at snow blowing from the submarine-stocked
trenches of the Baltic Sea,
and wondered how long I should stay.

Your country was at war with mine.
Its streets were cratered, mortar-shell gray,
its crowds raising their fists
before the blank-windowed embassies.
For the cameras they believed
in no other images but these.

Women in those crowds
were veiled, and under their veils
they'd erased their names, their faces
belonged to silence.

Beneath banners I could not read
I saw my life with you
in its black robes, backing away,
merging into shadows of doorways
where I would not be allowed to follow.

VII

To buy time, I rode south
to cities where copper-oxide domes
floated on the white marble cornices
of the Baroque. I walked
under amber fanlights, porcelain vaults
with gilded stucco fretwork
like inverted wedding cakes. I sat
in the Sacher-torte cafés, with conclusions
I kept avoiding. I thought
of all we would say, how I would struggle
to put the sentences together.

Each day, you told me,
you lived with the fear I was gone.
But I turned once again
between the checkpoints, the pistols
and dogs, back within reach
of your passport.

VIII

How did we linger so long?
Digits clicked off on our entry permits
while the dollar kept falling
in Bonn and Zürich, and I waited
for letters that refused to arrive,
to tell me it was time to go home.

But time held its breath
between us, and our old lives
were stories we told each other
in the dark. Only snow went on
tending its blooms in the courtyard.

You made good the years
I never gave myself, and I looked forward
to nights when it didn't matter
who we were: under the same sky
as every other traveller.
                                    Even the comet
streaking its one faintest chance across our lifetime
kept its word. No matter we never saw it.

What word did I keep,
nights that weariness refused me
and I hunched under the hotel lamp's
yellow stare, altering my ticket
to give myself one more month I didn't have
with you?
                    I thought of Rumi, searching
for the vanished Shams ud-Din, and knew
it was hopeless. My life was only

as much as it could be,
and when I asked why I couldn't leave
and couldn't stay, the answer
was too simple for me to bow my head.
My resolve froze, a majolica swan
stalled on a lake of sheet crystal
in a mad king's dream.

        IX

Then the port of Basra flared,
lotus flaming on the glazed oil slick
of the Tigris, and in the counterstrike
your brother fell among the mustard flowers'
choking blooms.

              For days you knew nothing,
only what voices—tiny and excited
in the long-distance receivers—didn't say.

We watched the television footage.
Boys writhing on cots in the medics' tents,
blood-froth on their lips
where breath crawled its collapsing tunnel
and your brother's face guttered out.

There was no way I could unspell
your sorrow. You would fly home
to pick up his flag. I understood then
how men cling to war
and women travel in the shadow
of other women's losses.

For days I shadowed you, office
to office, for papers they finally
stopped refusing.
                    Zürich then,
the refugee hotel, our last nights
filled with cooking smells
and children's voices in the halls.
Young men from your land, who were fleeing
what you sought. You'd memorized
all my midnight profiles, as if your hands,
drifting over my breasts in sleep,

could awaken us next morning
in your country. The light you left on
by the bed all night told me
you were already gone. Then
there was only the crowded station
of that nonaligned country
and your face among the others
receding from the platform.

X

I wandered between cathedral and museum,
the gray, eroded weight
of the late Gothic. I slept on narrow streets
by the central stations, in *pensiones*
with the names of women: ceiling fissures
the thin blue of veins, windows
the high, white squares of solitary.
I didn't know the future tense
of any language in which you could be held
at gunpoint for questioning.

How could I tell you
what I trusted? I
with my haphazard loves
and my talent for choosing badly.
Coin booths by the central *poste*
each night, our voices strung
on slackening wires across the hills,
the greening, damaged fields
beyond the Rhine.
                        You said
you were going back to Tabriz,
we would meet again in this country
we had never seen in summer.

There were late trains, necklaces of lights
to string the cities together
—Strasbourg, Paris, Brussels—
and planes lifting from tarmac
between the armored carriers'
flashing beams, troops with submachine guns
by the jetways, my luggage searched
and searched again.

XI

                              Behind me then
the splintered plate glass of Les Halles,
bodies scattered on a dance floor
in Berlin, the connection that clicked shut
in mid-sentence. For months
I searched the wire-service columns,
foolishly scanning the back paragraphs
for your name. From this continent
such a minor, distant conflict.

Each day arrived
with its instructive silence,
envelopes with familiar cancellations
like the face of a woman who thought
she was ready to face anything.

You were a cipher in a throwdown war,
a man behind barred windows
of a shop in Tehran, dropping
your account books, watching demonstrators
stab a young guard to the pavement,
his blood unstoppered in long,
guttering sobs—the lung-spurts
of an animal past helping.

Soldiers fired volley after volley
into the crowd, and you staggered
to the enclosed garden of your parents' house
thinking *This is not my country*.

XII

There is no country left
for the weaponless.
You who worked for weeks
to get a visa for one city,

and I, who ran my hands over the documents
I could not sign, that might have knotted
our countries' darkening strands together.
Our voices faded over sealed frontiers
in a language foreign to both of us,
hostages of the body's unsurrendered longings
and the Articles of War.

On this carpet with its dream-entangled flowers,
leopards and gazelles locked
in a struggle inevitable as death,
I cannot imagine our lives here,
our lives as they might have been otherwise.

Your beauty in its true languages
too dangerous: echo of the Great Mosque's geometry
and the infinite attributes of God,
one book that could almost be enough
for anyone.
                    Where you are now—
shop or cell or mountain bivouac
above villages whose names have been erased
by snow, the grief you were schooled in
beyond the reach

of letters I cannot write again.
That day you exhausted your store of rhymes,
your thoughts followed their deportation orders
and there was nothing but silence
left between us: woman and man
who could have been strangers once,
who never meant to go home unfinished.

Notes on the Poems

My Last Night in Bahia (pp. 3–5)
Capoeira is a ritualized martial-arts dance form evolved by slaves of African descent. Forbidden by their Brasilian masters to fight with their hands and upper bodies, slaves developed a system of standing on their hands and striking with their feet.

The *berimbāu* is a one-stringed folk instrument played with a plectrum, used to accompany *capoeira* players.

The Conjure Woman (pp. 6–7)
Bahia's principal religions are Catholicism and Candomblé, which originated in West Africa and whose deities have for the most part acquired counterparts among Catholic saints. Many people practice both religions. Yemanjá, the mermaid-like goddess of the sea and of Bahia's many fishermen, is honored on February 2 with net-pulling ceremonies, drinking, and dancing. Often her festivities coincide with those preceding Carnaval.

After Forty Years (pp. 9–10)
In June 1985, the body of Nazi death-camp doctor Josef Mengele was discovered in a grave in Embú, Brasil, where he had lived in hiding (with the knowledge of his family and many local people as to his identity) until his death by drowning. Embedded in his name is the German word *Engel*, angel. This irony was not lost on those who suffered and died at his hands.

The Miracle Room (pp. 11–12)
Nosso Senhor do Bomfim, the most popular of Bahia's many churches, is famed for the beauty of its colonial baroque architecture and for the healing power claimed for its namesake, Our Lord of Bomfim. The faithful have filled several rooms off the high altar with relics and mementos of miraculous cures, especially of physical deformities.

The Opening Up (pp. 17–18)
In the early 1970s, Brasil's ruling *junta*—embarrassed by the deterioration of cultural life after its exiling of prominent artists, musicians, and writers—permitted the less overtly political among them to return home. Gal Costa, Gilberto Gil, Maria Bethânia,

Dorival Caymmi, and Caetano Veloso are famous and beloved popular music stars in Brasil who have become better known in the past few years among listeners of jazz and Latin American "world" music in the United States.

Aymara Woman on Socabaya Street (pp. 22–23)

The silver mines of Potosí, legendary for their seemingly inexhaustible supplies of the precious ore, were exploited for four centuries by the Spanish conquerors of Bolivia. After the mines were depleted in the nineteenth century, tin—mined and sorted by native Aymara workers—continued to enrich the mine owners, descendants of the original colonists.

Eugenia (pp. 24–26)

Arauco, a coastal town in the province of the same name in the south of Chile, is still inhabited largely by people of Mapuche (Araucanian) descent. The Mapuches were never conquered by the Spanish colonizers' armies, but they lost much of their tribal land and culture through economic exploitation and discrimination after the Wars of Conquest ended in the late nineteenth century.

"*Arbolé, arbolé, seco y verdé*" is the refrain of Federico García Lorca's poem, "Arbolé, arbolé," from his book *Canciones* (1921–24).

Dawson Island, in the far southern archipelago region of Chile, was the site of an internment camp for political dissidents established after the military coup of September 1973.

Violeta Parra, one of Chile's best-known and beloved folk musicians and poets, composed many songs on social and political conditions, especially the plight of the poor. The epigraph, from her song "Arauco tiene una pena," is paraphrased in the poem's last stanza.

Victor Jara (1932–1973) (pp. 28–29)

The torture and murder of Victor Jara in one of Santiago's national soccer stadiums a few days after the military coup shocked the world, and Jara himself became a symbol of the power of song for political and social change. For most of the Pinochet regime's seventeen years in power, Jara's work—along with that of Violeta Parra, her children Angel and Isabel, and other musical groups of the Chilean New Song movement such as Inti-Illimani and Quilapayún—was banned in Chile, and people risked their lives to play it. Many of these musicians survived arrest and imprisonment, escaped to spend the Pinochet years in exile, and returned to Chile only after the 1990 restoration of democracy.

Santiago has two big outdoor stadiums, the Estadio Nacional and the Estadio Chile, both of which were used as detention and torture centers after the coup. It was first announced that Victor had been detained and killed in the Estadio Nacional, hence the mention of this site in the poem, but this information turned out to be incorrect. He had died in the Estadio Chile.

On September 11, 2003, the thirtieth anniversary of the military coup in Chile, a huge commemorative concert was held in this stadium featuring many musicians of Chile's New Song movement and their descendants, as well as other returned exiles and survivors of Pinochet's years of oppression. To honor and preserve the memory of those who had died and disappeared after the coup, at that concert the Estadio Chile was officially renamed the Estadio Victor Jara.

Sierra Walk   (pp. 32–33)

Ollantaitambo (the name means "fertile field") was one of the major agricultural centers of the late Inca Empire and also boasted some of the finest examples of Inca stone masonry outside of Cuzco. Many of the fitted-stone hill terraces constructed at that time are still used for growing maize and potatoes by the Quechua people—whom the Peruvians of European descent called *cholos,* a contemptuous term for the indigenous inhabitants whose land and wealth were stolen by the Spanish conquerors.

Coplas for Violeta Parra (1917–1967)   (pp. 41–43)

Multitalented Violeta Parra spent her life collecting and arranging traditional folk songs and dances from throughout Chile, composing and performing her own songs—often accompanied by her son and daughter Angel and Isabel—painting and sculpting, and embroidering the brilliant *arpilleras* (tapestries), exhibited in the Louvre in 1964, for which she is as renowned in Chile as she is for her music. But little recognition came during her lifetime, and in February 1967, despondent over financial and personal matters, Violeta Parra took her own life.

The former Peña de los Parra, the folk music club that she founded with Isabel and Angel in 1965, was boarded up and abandoned during the Pinochet years, but it is now an important Santiago gallery and performing arts center, the Centro Cultural Violeta Parra.

The epigraph, by her elder brother, poet Nicanor Parra, is from his "Defensa de Violeta Parra."

KZ   (pp. 44–45)

"*KZ*" is the German abbreviation for *Konzentrationslager*.
This poem is for Terrence Des Pres, 1939–1987.

The Room   (pp. 49–51)

For several days after the September 11, 1973, coup in which the
elected government of Salvador Allende was overthrown, spokesmen
for the new military regime claimed that the dead president had
committed suicide in his office during the aerial bombardment of
the Moneda, the presidential palace. The suicide weapon was alleged
to be a submachine gun presented to Allende by Fidel Castro during
the Cuban leader's visit to Chile in December 1971.

Later, however, journalists and other eyewitnesses present when
the president's body was removed from the Moneda asserted that he
died in combat when soldiers burst into his office after storming the
bomb-gutted building. Allende's widow, Hortensia Bussi de Allende,
who had originally believed the suicide story, agreed with this newer
version of events after seeing photos of her husband's bullet-riddled
corpse. In 1990, however, when Allende's body was finally removed
from an unmarked grave and given proper burial, further examination
once again seemed to indicate that the besieged president may indeed
have taken his own life.

I am indebted to Margaret Gibson, R. N., who narrated to me the
events upon which this poem is based and who gave her permission
for them to appear in this poetic form, and to the *New York Times*
of September 12–26, 1973, for reports that provided corroborating
information.

The Peace Corps Volunteer Comes Home   (p. 52)

Feijoada, a sort of stew of black beans with rice, is the staple diet
of Brasil's poor. Recife is the principal port of the sugar-cane growing
region in the northeast.

A *figa* is an amulet shaped like a clenched fist, with the thumb
protruding from between the first and middle fingers.

Message to César Vallejo   (pp. 53–54)

This poem grew out of reading *César Vallejo: The Complete
Posthumous Poetry* (University of California Press, 1978), translated by
Clayton Eshleman and José Rubia Barcia. Eshleman's introduction to
the book was the source for details of the Peruvian poet's life.

Josie Bliss, October 1971   (pp. 55–57)

In 1927–28, the young Pablo Neruda, Chilean consul to Burma, lived in Rangoon with a native woman who dressed in English clothing and used the name "Josie Bliss" in public. According to Neruda's account in his memoir, *Confieso que he vivido* (translated as *Memoirs* by Hardie St. Martin; Farrar, Straus & Giroux, 1977), Josie Bliss suffered from fits of jealous rage based on the correct presentiment that he would eventually leave her.

Transferred to Ceylon, Neruda departed in secret; but Josie Bliss managed to trace and follow him, appearing one day in the yard of his house in Colombo (which he was already, his memoir informs us, sharing with "a sweet Eurasian girl"). Only after many scenes and visits from the police did Neruda persuade Josie Bliss to go home. She departed tearfully, and he never saw her again.

Thirty years later, Neruda visited Burma with his third and final wife, Matilde Urrutia. He looked, but could find "not a trace" of Josie Bliss, nor even of the Rangoon neighborhood where they had lived. He continued to write poems about her all his life.

In October of 1971, Pablo Neruda won the Nobel Prize for Literature. The announcement was carried by newspapers all over the world. If Josie Bliss were still alive then, she would undoubtedly have seen it.

The epigraph is from Neruda's own "Josie Bliss," the final poem in his early book, *Residencia en la tierra (1921–31)*.

Flowers in Winter   (pp. 61–71)

Isfahan is a style of carpet weaving named for the city in central Iran where it originated; it is noted for its delicate floral and mythological animal designs. Knots in the finest carpets are so small and tight that hundreds are needed for a square inch, and weavers are said to go blind at an early age from their work.

Hafiz (c. 1300–1388) and Saadi (c. 1184–1291), both natives of the city of Shiraz, were two of the most popular and prolific poets of the classical period of Persian literature.

"Throne of Thrones" was one title of the last Shah of Iran, Mohammed Reza Pahlavi, deposed in 1979 by the Islamic fundamentalist party led by the Ayatollah Khomeini.

Jalal ud-Din Rumi (1207–1273) was a Persian theologian and Koranic scholar in the Seljuk capital of Konya in central Turkey, who in early middle age came under the influence of a wandering dervish, Shams ud-Din of Tabriz. Jalal ud-Din took the mysterious stranger into his house, and for several years he and the "hidden saint" were inseparable. But threats of violence from the scholar's jealous disciples and students caused the dervish twice to flee to Damascus, and on the second of these journeys Shams vanished without a trace.

Transformed by his passion from a sober theologian to an ecstasy-filled devotee, Rumi never ceased to grieve for his lost friend, and for the rest of his life poured out extemporaneous lyrics and quatrains while in states of mystical transport—poetry that his disciples transcribed on the spot and memorized. In these poems, he named Shams ud-Din as the Beloved, the source of his inspiration; and the search for the vanished earthly beloved became symbolic of the quest for union with the ineffable Divine. Rumi's transformation caused his solid scholarly reputation to give way to popular fame, and his circle of disciples grew, so that in his last years he presided over his own Mevlevi Order of Dervishes, while composing the works that made him one of the most prolific mystical poets of all time.

A large Nymphenburg majolica vase in the shape of a swan, the favorite animal of "mad" King Ludwig II of Bavaria, still stands in the "swan corner" of the living room of his fabulous castle, Neuschwanstein.

Basra, the Iraqi oil refinery and port on the Tigris River near the Persian Gulf, was heavily damaged in a surprise attack by Iranian troops in late January 1986. In the counterattack, Iraqi troops used poison mustard gas, killing or wounding several hundred Iranian soldiers.

Sources for details of the lives of Persian poets named here are *The Reader's Companion to World Literature* (New American Library, 1956), edited by Lillian Hornstein, G. D. Percy, and Calvin S. Brown; *The Reader's Encyclopedia* (2nd edition), edited by William Rose Benét (Thomas Y. Crowell, 1965); and A. J. Arberry's introduction to his classic translation, *Discourses of Rumi* (John Murray, 1961).

About the Author

Carolyne Wright studied at Seattle University and New York University and holds masters and doctoral degrees in English and creative writing from Syracuse University. She has published eight books and chapbooks of poetry, including *Premonitions of an Uneasy Guest* (AWP Award Series) and *From a White Woman's Journal* (Water Mark Press); a collection of essays; and three volumes of poetry in translation from Spanish and Bengali.

She has received awards for her writing from the Poetry Society of America, the NEA, and the New York State Council on the Arts, and she has held writing fellowships in poetry at the Fine Arts Work Center in Provincetown, the Vermont Studio Center, and Yaddo. Translation editor for *Artful Dodge*, she serves on the board of directors of the Association of Writers and Writing Programs (AWP). A visiting poet and professor at colleges, universities, and writers' conferences throughout the United States and in other countries, Wright recently moved back to her native Seattle, where she teaches in the Whidbey Writers' Workshop MFA program and for the Richard Hugo House.

Acknowledgments

Grateful acknowledgment goes to the following periodicals in which these poems, sometimes in earlier versions, first appeared:

Apalachee Quarterly: "Wander Luís"

Black Warrior Review: "Message to César Vallejo," "Josie Bliss, October 1971"

Brilliant Corners: "The Opening Up, 1972"

The Cream City Review: "*Sierra* Walk"

Denver Quarterly: "Survivor's Story" (as "A High Wind Through Your Life")

The Georgia Review: "Survivalist" (as "The Mythology of Guns")

Green Mountains Review: "Harumi"

Image: "*KZ*"

The Iowa Review: "The Room"

Iron Horse Literary Review: "La Push," "Harumi"

Lullwater Review: "Survivor's Story"

Ms. Magazine: "The Grade School Teacher During Recess"

New Letters: "After Forty Years"

Nimrod: Section VIII of "Flowers in Winter"

Open Places: "The Miracle Room," "The Peace Corps Volunteer Comes Home"

Ploughshares: "The Retarded Woman on Cooper Street"

Poet Lore: "Flowers in Winter"

Poetry Society of America Newsletter: "*KZ*," "Message to César Vallejo," "Josie Bliss, October 1971"

Quarterly West: "Aymara Woman on Socabaya Street"

Sundog: "*Sierra* Walk"

Willow Springs: "My Last Night in Bahia"

Witness: "Wander Luís" (as "Talking Politics").

"Victor Jara (1932–1973)" and "Post-Revolutionary Letter" first appeared in *Poetry* (© The Modern Poetry Association).

Acknowledgment is also due to the following anthologies:

New American Poets of the 80's (Wampeter Press, 1984): "Josie Bliss, October 1971"; *Blood to Remember: American Poets on the Holocaust* (Texas Tech University Press, 1991): "After Forty Years," "*KZ*"; *And What Rough Beast: Poems at the End of the Century* (Ashland Poetry Press, 1999): "The Peace Corps Volunteer Comes Home"; *Poets of the New Century* (David R. Godine, 2001): "The Room," "The Conjure Woman"; *Like Thunder: Poets Respond to Violence in America* (University of Iowa Press, 2001): "Survivalist"; *Range of Voices: A Collection of Contemporary Poets* (Eastern Washington University Press, 2005): "My Last Night in Bahia," "The Conjure Woman," "*Sierra* Walk," "Post-Revolutionary Letter," "KZ."

Several of these poems previously appeared in the chapbook *From a White Woman's Journal* (Water Mark Press, 1985; 2nd printing, 1994): "The Conjure Woman,"

"The Miracle Room," "Eugenia," "The Peace Corps Volunteer Comes Home," "Message to César Vallejo," "Josie Bliss, October 1971."

"Message to César Vallejo" received the Celia B. Wagner Award from the Poetry Society of America.

"Josie Bliss, October 1971" received the John Masefield Memorial Award for a Narrative Poem from the Poetry Society of America.

"*KZ*" received the Lucille Medwick Memorial Award from the Poetry Society of America and an Honorable Mention from *The Pushcart Prize XV: Best of the Small Presses* (1990).

"Wander Luís" was a second-place winner of the *Apalachee Quarterly* Long Poem Award.

"My Last Night in Bahia" received the Erika Mumford Prize from the New England Poetry Club.

"Flowers in Winter" received the John Williams Andrews Narrative Poetry Prize from *Poet Lore* and the Milton Dorfman Poetry Prize from the Rome Arts and Community Center.

I wish to thank the Comisión Fulbright of Chile and the Institute of International Education for the Fulbright-Hays Study Grant which first took me to Chile and made possible the experiences on which a number of these poems are based. I am also grateful to the Mary Ingraham Bunting Institute of Radcliffe College, the Centrum Foundation, the Creative Artists Public Service (CAPS) Program of New York State, the Fine Arts Work Center in Provincetown, the National Endowment for the Arts, the National Endowment for the Humanities, the Seattle Arts Commission, and the Corporation of Yaddo for fellowships and grants that provided support while I was working on this book.

Special thanks to friends who read these poems and gave suggestions and encouragement, particularly Marjorie Agosín, Tim Bryson, Teresa Cader, Christopher Jane Corkery, Ha Jin, Yusef Komunyakaa, Stephanie Painter, Roger Weingarten, and Deborah Woodard.